# ANDREW PEACOCK'S RUMBLING TUM

Cottage Publishing

*Published in Great Britain 1995 by*
Cottage Publishing, Bovey Tracey, Devon
Tel: 01626  835757

*Designed & Typeset by*
Cottage Publishing, Bovey Tracey, Devon

*Photographs by*
Bim, Bovey Tracey, Devon

*Illustrations by*
Adrian Peacock

*Printed by*
Sprint Print, Exeter

British Library Cataloguing in Publication Data
CIP Catalogue Record for this book is available from the British Library
ISBN 1 897785 04 6

# Foreword

by

**The Earl of Iddesleigh DL**

*Chairman of the Gemini Charitable Trust*

I am very pleased indeed to be given the opportunity to write a few words in preface to this excellent book. The recipes to be found here and the menus they make up are truly representative of the excellent cooking, ambience and value for money that customers of the Rumbling Tum have come to expect.

On behalf of the Trustees of the Gemini Charitable Trust and those local charities and individuals that the Trust has been set up to benefit, I thank Andrew and Frances Peacock for their generosity in both compiling and funding the publication of this book so that the maximum possible proportion of the cover price is able to be devoted to those within Devon whose need for help is greatest.

I should also like to thank Steve Browning of Gemini Radio who, together with Andrew and Frances, conceived the idea and whose conversations with Andrew on the Morning Show have kept us amused and informed so vividly on matters culinary.

Please recommend this book to your friends.

# CONTENTS

# INTRODUCTION

L et me introduce myself to you - I am Andrew Peacock, and together with my wife, Frances, I have been running the Rumbling Tum Restaurant in Bovey Tracey since 1982. I trained initially as a chef in my home town of Guildford, Surrey, and served my apprenticeship in Restaurant Movenpick in Geneva, Switzerland. It is there that I learnt about the importance of attention to detail, and acquired a passion for desserts and patisserie, serving for some time in the position of pastry chef.

The Rumbling Tum is a 15th century restaurant in the centre of Bovey Tracey, with many medieval features - the huge studded door, original oak screens, granite fireplaces, and beams galore, all of which help to create an intimate atmosphere. Our aim here is to create for our customers an evening to remember.

During my time at the Rumbling Tum, I have often been frustrated at being unable to obtain some of the more unusual fresh herbs and salads, and I have now established a herb/salad/fruit garden solely for supplying the restaurant. I would suggest that every vegetable garden should have a corner devoted to herbs such as lovage, sorrel, chervil, coriander, tarragon and fennel.

One of the most important elements in creating any dish is to use the best quality ingredients you can afford. Where, in any recipe, there are short cuts to achieving a certain taste, I will advise you of them. Do not be tempted to substitute an ingredient with something of an inferior nature. Do not, as a customer once did when following one of my recipes, replace a glass of Tia Maria with a glass of sherry, and then wonder why it didn't taste the same! All the menus have been formulated with a dinner party for four people in mind.

I am so pleased to be associated with Steve Browning of Gemini AM, - politician, broadcaster and restaurateur in his own right, who was the inspiration behind this publication. From the outset, it had been our intention to offer the profits to a local charitable cause, and it, therefore, seemed appropriate to involve the Gemini Charitable Trust, who will be distributing the proceeds to projects in the locality.

It has been my great pleasure to share with you this collection of recipes that I have been serving over the years at the Rumbling Tum, and that have become favourites with my customers. I hope that you enjoy using them to entertain your friends.

Andrew Peacock
Rumbling Tum Restaurant
68 Fore Street
Bovey Tracey
Devon
Tel: 01626 832543

# MENU 1

## Avocado Seafood Melange

## Venison with Mushrooms & Garlic

## Nectarine Sorbet

The Melange came about as a happy accident one Sunday evening, when, whilst relaxing, I felt a bit peckish. A trip to the fridge revealed some leftovers - prawns, smoked trout, Brie, avocado, grapes and mayonnaise. I gathered them up, put them in a dish, added some crushed nuts - and found that the result was a wonderful mingling of flavours and textures - the smokiness of the fish, the smooth avocado, the sharpness of the grapes, and the soft texture of the Brie. By the next weekend, Avocado Seafood Melange (the name took longer to devise than the dish!) featured on the restaurant menu, and has done so ever since, being by far and away the most popular starter I have ever served.

Venison is now more widely available than a few years ago, as there are now many farms rearing deer. It is a very lean meat, and, provided it is not overcooked, will be the texture more of paté than meat. I recommend a strong red wine to partner this course - try an Italian Barolo.

Nectarine Sorbet is a light dessert to end this meal, and could be served with almond biscuits and a glass of Amaretto liqueur.

## AVOCADO SEAFOOD MELANGE

**6 oz prawns**
**2 small smoked trout fillets, flaked**
**4 tbsp. mayonnaise**
**1 ripe avocado, cut into rough dice**
**1 small bunch seedless grapes, halved**
**4 oz Brie, cut into $^1/_2$" cubes**
**1 doz. roasted hazelnuts, crushed**
**1 small rosso lettuce**
**cucumber, tomato and cress, to garnish**

Take 4 decorative glass dishes or bowls, and arrange a few rosso lettuce leaves around the edge. Divide the prawns, smoked trout and avocado between the dishes, and cover with mayonnaise. Sprinkle the Brie and grapes on top and toss the roasted hazelnuts over. Decorate with a twist of cucumber, tomato segment and cress.

***CHEF'S TIP*** *Do not leave your hazelnuts roasting under the grill unattended, as they will easily burn. Now is not the time to make a quick phone call!*

## VENISON WITH MUSHROOMS AND GARLIC

**4 x 6 oz venison steaks (cut from the haunch)**
**12 cloves garlic, peeled**
**1/2 pt chicken stock**
**4 oz button mushrooms, sliced**
**4 oz double cream**
**salt and pepper**
**to garnish -**
**2 rashers smoked bacon**
**4 sliced mushrooms**

Sauce: Take the garlic cloves, and blanch them three times for two minutes each time - using fresh water. Take the chicken stock, add the garlic cloves and sliced button mushrooms and cook for 5 minutes. Blend to a smooth purée in a liquidizer. Return to the pan, reheat and add the cream. Adjust the seasoning.

Saute the steaks for approx. 3 minutes each side, according to taste.

**To serve** - divide the sauce between 4 plates and place one steak on each. Lightly fry the garnish of mushrooms and bacon, finely dice and sprinkle over.

## NECTARINE SORBET

**7 oz sugar**
**$^1/_2$ cinnamon stick (or 1 tsp. powdered cinnamon)**
**4 tbsp. water**
**juice of 1 lemon**
**juice of 1 lime**
**1 $^1/_4$ lb nectarines (to yield 17 fl oz purée)**

Bring the sugar, cinnamon and water to the boil. Leave to cool and strain. Stir the lime and lemon juice into the fruit purée and mix into the cold syrup. Freeze the sorbet, remove after 30 minutes and stir thoroughly. Repeatedly freeze and stir, to ensure that the sorbet is smooth.

*CHEF'S TIP* - *as nectarines vary in sweetness, extra lime or lemon juice may be required.*

# MENU 2

## Friar's Utter Bliss

## Salmon with Scallops

## Oeufs à la Neige

This menu was compiled with an elegant dinner party on a warm summer's evening in mind.

The starter is refreshing and light, and very attractive served in a sugared glass - dip the rim in egg white and then caster sugar. Guests need to be seated at the table and the starter assembled at the last minute and carried immediately to the table. Better still, top off with the sparkling wine at the table.

Salmon with Scallops is a luxurious main course, and the expense of the latter is outweighed by the very good value of the former. The grapes add a certain sharpness to the dish, and I would suggest a good Australian Chardonnay to complement this course.

Oeufs à la Neige (or Snow Eggs) are a personal favourite of mine - a reminder of nursery food!

## FRIAR'S UTTER BLISS

**1 large or 2 small melons**
**8 oz strawberries**
**2 tsp brandy**
**4 tbsp icing sugar**
**1/2 lb fresh cherries**
**1/2 bottle sparkling white wine**

Liquidize the strawberries with the brandy and sugar and chill. Divide the balled melon and stoned cherries between 4 sugared glass dishes. Pour the strawberry purée over the fruit and add the sparkling wine at the last moment.

## SALMON WITH SCALLOPS

4 escalopes of salmon (6 - 8 oz)  
4 tbsp butter  
1 oz chopped walnuts  
2 oz seedless green grapes  

8 scallops, sliced  
1 tbsp lemon juice  
salt and freshly ground pepper  

Take a frying pan large enough to hold the 4 salmon pieces in a single layer, and heat 2 tbsp of the butter. Add the salmon and saute for 2 - 3 minutes each side, over a gentle heat. Transfer to a warmed plate, and keep warm. Add the remaining butter to the pan, and toss the walnuts, grapes and scallops briefly - about 1 minute - the scallops should by now be opaque. Season, and spoon the mixture over the salmon.

*CHEF'S TIP - ask your fishmonger for escalopes of salmon rather than steaks, as these will cook more evenly, result in a better presentation, and you will find little or no bones.*

## OEUFS À LA NEIGE

8 eggs, separated  
1³/4 pts milk  
7 oz caster sugar  
2 tsp. vanilla essence  
2 oz flaked toasted almonds  

Caramel -  
  4 oz granulated sugar  
  2 tbsp water  
  3 - 4 tbsp almond liqueur  
  (optional)  

Prepare the caramel by placing the water in a thick-bottomed pan, adding the sugar and allowing to boil gently, without shaking or stirring the pan. When the sugar has cooked to a golden brown colour, add the almond liqueur (or alternatively 3 - 4 tbsp water), reboil and set aside to cool.

Take the egg whites and beat with 2 oz of the caster sugar until firm. Heat the milk in a large pan until it is just simmering. Take 2 soup spoons and shape the meringue into balls. Drop the shapes into the milk and poach briefly - 20 seconds on one side, and 10 seconds on the other. Remove and set aside to cool - the balls should be the consistency of soft marsh- mallows. Retain the milk. Beat the egg yolks, 5 oz caster sugar and vanilla essence and whisk in the milk used for poaching. Make a custard of this mixture by either - a) stirring over a low heat in a pan until the custard coats the spoon, or b) using a microwave on a low setting or defrost, stirring occasionally. Pour the custard into a shallow serving dish to cool. Arrange the marshmallows in a pyramid shape on top of the custard, scatter the almonds over and pour the caramel on top, so that it cascades down the sides.

*CHEF'S TIP - if you are not confident about making caramel, you can buy it pre-prepared from your supermarket.*

# MENU 3

## Avocado Pepper

## Fennel and Mushrooms

## Plum and Honey Mousse

This menu was devised to suit the vegetarian, and the starter, which is an avocado with a filling of sweet red pepper and mushroom duxelle topped with a pinenut crumble, can become a main course by using 2 halves of avocado per portion and with the addition of a parsley sauce.

Fennel is a vegetable that I always enjoy using. It has a lovely aniseed flavour, which is such a surprise to anyone who has never tasted it before. Serve this main course on a bed of rice, and accompany it with a glass of Muscadet.

The dessert, a light and fluffy mousse, combines the sharpness of plums with the mellow sweetness of honey.

## AVOCADO PEPPER

**2 avocados, halved and stoned**
**2 oz diced red pepper**
**7 tsp butter**
**6 oz mushrooms, finely chopped**
**2 oz onion, finely chopped**
**2 oz breadcrumbs**
**2 oz grated cheddar cheese**
**1 handful pinenuts**

Cut a very thin slice off the bottom of each half of avocado so that it will sit flat. Sweat together the red pepper and 2 tsp of the butter in a pan or microwave. Cook the mushrooms and onion in a further teaspoon of butter. Mix the mushroom and red pepper together and mound onto the advocados. Melt the remaining butter, add the breadcrumbs and cheese and bind together. Press the crumble firmly onto the avocado, reshaping into the original avocado shape. Press the pinenuts into the crumble, place in a microwave for 2 minutes to warm through and finish off under the grill.

*CHEF'S TIP - try to use white mushrooms for the duxelle to avoid the mixture becoming too dark.*

6

## FENNEL AND MUSHROOMS

1 lb fennel, finely sliced
2 lb mushrooms, sliced
8 oz onions, finely chopped
4 tbsp parsley, finely chopped
2 tbsp fennel fronds, chopped
6 oz butter
6 tbsp plain flour
16 fl oz milk
salt and freshly ground pepper

Melt half the butter in a saucepan, stir in the flour and cook for a few minutes over a very low heat. Remove from the heat and add the milk slowly, stirring until smooth. Return to the heat and simmer, stirring, for 5 minutes, until thick. Meanwhile, melt the rest of the butter in a frying pan, and add the fennel, mushrooms, onion and fronds. Season, cover and simmer for 8 - 10 minutes, by which time the vegetables should be tender. Add the sauce and simmer for a further 2 - 3 minutes.

## PLUM AND HONEY MOUSSE

juice of 1 lemon
1/2 oz powdered gelatine
14 oz cooking plums, halved and stoned
3 fl oz pure apple juice
2 eggs, separated
3 tbsp clear honey
1/2 tsp cinnamon
5 fl oz double cream, whipped
to garnish - 2 tbsp chopped walnuts

Add the gelatine to the lemon juice in a small bowl, and melt slowly in the microwave on defrost. Cook the plums in the apple juice until soft. Liquidize and sieve into a saucepan. Over a low heat, add the honey and stir until dissolved. Remove from heat, stir the dissolved gelatine into the purée. Beat in the egg yolks, return the pan to a low heat and stir until it coats the back of a spoon - without letting it boil. Cool and chill for approx 30 minutes - until almost set. Whisk the egg whites. Fold the whipped cream and then the egg whites into the purée and divide between individual glasses. Decorate with the chopped nuts.

*CHEF'S TIP* - *when preparing gelatine, make sure it is all well soaked before heating.*

# MENU 4

**Somerset Onion Soup**

**Beef Wellington**

**Pears in Cassis**

Menu 5 would especially suit a chilly autumn evening - a warming soup, a substantial main course, and a light, fruity yet elegant dessert.

The soup is similar to the traditional french onion soup, but given a local twist with the addition of dry cider.

This particular beef wellington is cooked in individual portions, using a mushroom duxelle rather than pate. A Madeira or Red Wine Sauce would go well with this dish, and I would suggest a Crozes Hermitage as a wine to complement it.

The dessert, pears in a blackcurrant sauce with cassis liqueur, definitely improves with the keeping, as the fruit takes on more and more of the flavour and colour of the marinade. I have allowed 2 pears per portion, as you will find that when you have eaten one, you want to eat another!

## SOMERSET ONION SOUP

**1 lb onions (sliced)**
**2 tbsp butter**
**2 pt brown stock**
**2 tbsp cornflour**

Sweat the onions with the butter in a saucepan with a lid until they are slightly coloured, but not burnt. Add the cider and stock and cook for 10 minutes. Mix the cornflour to a paste with a little water and stir into the soup. Cook for a further few minutes.

## BEEF WELLINGTON

| | |
|---|---|
| 4 x 4 - 5 oz fillet steaks | 1 $^1/_2$ lb puff pastry |
| 1 lb mushrooms (finely chopped) | 1 egg |
| 4 oz onion (finely chopped) | salt and pepper |
| 2 oz butter | |

Make a duxelle by sweating the onion in the butter until soft, add the mushroom and a little seasoning and cook over a low heat, stirring occasionally to allow the mixture to dry. Preheat the oven to 250C/475F/Gas 8 or 9. Take the fillet steaks and seal each side in hot fat briefly. Roll the puff pastry out into 8 x 5" diameter circles. Place one tablespoon of the duxelle on 4 of the circles and place the fillets on top. Add a further tablespoon of duxelle on the top of each fillet, egg wash the edge of the pastry and cover with the remaining circles of pastry. Seal the edges well, egg wash, and make a small incision on the top of each to allow steam to escape. Cook in the oven for 15 - 20 minutes, depending to which stage you wish your steak cooked - 15 minutes for rate, 20 minutes for medium.

*CHEF'S TIP - when initially sealing the steaks, cook only briefly on each side- it is not the intention to cook the steak at this stage, but merely to seal in the juices.*

## PEARS IN CASSIS

| | |
|---|---|
| 8 ripe but firm pears | 1 tsp cinnamon |
| 1 pt red wine | squeeze of lemon juice |
| 1 lb blackcurrants | 4 - 6 tbsp cassis |
| 1/4 pt water | cornflour to thicken, as necessary |
| 8 oz caster sugar | |

Cook the blackcurrants in the water with the sugar until soft. Liquidize and sieve. Peel the pears very carefully to retain their shape, and without removing the stalk. Place them gently into a saucepan, and add the wine, the blackcurrant purée, cinnamon and lemon juice. Poach gently until tender - 10 - 15 minutes according to size. Test with a small knife - which you should be able to insert to the core without resistance. Remove the pears. Reduce the purée, and thicken with a little cornflour, if necessary. Lastly add the cassis liqueur. Pour the sauce over the pears, chill and leave to marinade, turning the pears carefully occasionally. To serve, place 2 pears upright in each serving dish and pour the sauce over.

*CHEF'S TIP - Williams or Comice pears are ideal for this dish - we are looking for a real pear-shape, therefore care should be taken in choosing them, and especially when peeling them - we do not want to end up with pears that are more the shape of potatoes. You may need to cut the smallest slice off the end of each pear before serving so that it will stand up straight.*

# MENU 5

## Stuffed Peach

## Rabbit in White Wine & Mustard

## White Chocolate Ice Cream

Lhe stuffed peach has to be my all-time favourite starter. The mingling of the flavours - garlic, cream cheese and peach, is exquisite. The only disadvantage to this dish is that peaches are available for such a short season - smaller ones may be available for a longer season, but you must wait for the large ones for this starter.

Rabbit is, of course, a very lean meat, with less cholesterol than chicken, and it makes a very reasonably-priced main course. Ask you butcher for leg and saddle portions.

The presentation of the dessert is very elegant, and the contrast of dark bitter chocolate and hazelnuts on the base, with the smooth white chocolate and Drambuie ice-cream, offset by the sharpness of the red fruit sauce, is quite divine.

## STUFFED PEACH

**4 large, ripe peaches**
**8 oz soft cream cheese**
**2 cloves garlic (finely chopped)**
**1 tsp dried parsley**
**4 slices of 3" x 3" cheddar cheese (1/4" thick)**

Combine the cream cheese with the garlic and parsley. Halve and stone the peaches, and fill the stone cavity with the cheese mixture. Firm the 2 halves back together. Place a slice of cheddar on each peach. Warm for 1 minute in the microwave, and finish off under the grill, until the cheese has melted.

*CHEF'S TIP - you may prefer to buy the garlic cream cheese pre-prepared from your delicatessen or supermarket.*

10

## RABBIT IN WHITE WINE AND MUSTARD

4 rabbit portions
2 small onions (chopped)
2 cloves garlic (chopped)
4 oz bacon (chopped)
1 pt dry white wine
$^1/_2$ pt chicken stock thyme, parsley
& bayleaf

grated rind and juice 1 lemon 2
tbsp flour
2 oz butter
2 egg yolks
4 oz double cream
2 dstsp mustard

Take the rabbit joints, season, flour and fry in butter until golden, to seal. Place in casserole dish. Fry the chopped onion and bacon, and stir in the flour. Add the white wine and stock, mix well and pour over the rabbit joints in the casserole. Add a sprinkling of parsley and thyme, bayleaf, the chopped garlic, and the juice and zest of the lemon. Cover and cook gently in the oven 150C/300F Mark 2. Before serving, make a liaison of the egg yolks, double cream and mustard and stir into the casserole.

## WHITE CHOCOLATE ICE-CREAM

8 fl oz white chocolate
4 fl oz double cream
3 tbsp Drambuie
2 eggs, separated
Bases - 3 oz dark chocolate
2 oz shelled hazelnuts
(toasted and chopped)
1 fl oz double cream

Sauce - $^1/_2$ lb raspberries or
redcurrants
2 oz caster sugar
squeeze of lemon juice
1 fl oz water

Melt the white chocolate in a bowl over a pan of hot water. Remove from the heat. Add 1 oz of the double cream and the liqueur and whisk in. Allow to cool for 5 minutes. Whisk in the 2 egg yolks. Whisk the remaining 3 oz cream and fold into the cooled mixture. Whisk the egg whites until stiff but not dry and fold in until smooth. Divide the mixture between 4 ramekin dishes and freeze.

Bases - melt the dark chocolate as previously. Remove from the heat and add the double cream, stirring thoroughly. Add the hazelnuts and divide between 4 individual greaseproofed flan tins, a little larger in diameter than the ramekin dishes used for the ice-ceam. Refrigerate until set. Turn out.

Sauce - cook, liquidize and sieve the fruit, sugar, lemon juice and water.

To assemble - take 4 decorative plates. Place one base on each, and pour a little sauce to the side. Run the outside of each ramekin briefly under the hot tap and turn out onto the bases. Decorate with curls of white chocolate.

*CHEF'S TIP - when melting the white chocolate, if this tends to solidify, add a tablespoon of boiling water and stir in, and this will return the mixture to the correct consistency. To make chocolate curls - warm the bar of chocolate briefly in the microwave and use a potato peeler to scrape.*

11

# MENU 6

## Mermaid's Pillow

## Chicken with Mushroom & Ginger

## Lemon & Vodka Meringue Cake

M ermaid's Pillow is scampi cooked in vermouth and cream and served in a pillow of puff pastry, with a julienne of carrot and celery.

The main course - chicken breast stuffed with mushroom and fresh ginger, served with an orange and crème fraîche sauce, is well worth the effort, but not to be attempted if you are in a hurry!

Lemon and Vodka Meringue Cake is layers of meringue, a rich lemon custard, and vodka cream. For presentation, if you should be able to find a yellow rose in the garden, this would look quite spectacular placed on top of the dessert.

## MERMAID'S PILLOW

**4 puff pastry rectangles, 3" x 2"**
**4 fl oz fish stock**
**8 fl oz dry vermouth**
**20 scampi**
**8 fl oz whipping cream**
**$^1/_2$ tsp dried tarragon**
**2 oz each julienne strips of celery and carrot**
**1 tbsp butter**
**1 squeeze lemon juice**

Cook the pastry rectangles. Cut in half horizontally and keep warm. Heat the fish stock and vermouth together, add the cream and reduce. Mix in the tarragon, butter and lemon juice. Meanwhile take the celery and carrot and cut into thin strips about the size of matchsticks, and blanch in water until tender. Poach the scampi in the vermouth sauce. Place the bottom half of each pastry onto your serving plates, add the scampi and sauce, and the vegetable matchsticks. Put the pastry tops on and serve immediately.

*CHEF'S TIP - take care not to overcook the scampi, or they will become tough and rubbery.*

## CHICKEN WITH MUSHROOM AND GINGER

4 chicken breasts, skinned and boned
6 oz mushrooms (finely chopped)
1 tbsp onions (finely chopped)
1 tbsp fresh ginger root (grated)
salt and freshly ground pepper
12 fl oz chicken stock

4 fl oz crème fracîhe
grated peel of 2 oranges
$^1/_4$ pt orange juice
1 tbsp sugar
3 tbsp white wine vinegar
Garnish - 1 orange, peeled and segmented

Make a duxelle of the mushrooms and onions, as in recipe 5. Add the grated ginger and cook for a further 2 minutes, season. Cut a slit in each of the chicken breasts and fill with the duxelle. Use a cocktail stick to secure. Put the orange juice, sugar and orange peel into a heavy pan and reduce to a light syrup. Add the wine vinegar and simmer. Add the stock and simmer until reduced. Cook the chicken breasts in a pan with a little butter and oil, lid on, over a very low heat, 8 - 10 minutes. Lift out the chicken breasts and place on a warmed serving dish. Warm the orange segments. Reheat the sauce and stir in the crème fraîche. Pour over the chicken and garnish with the oranges.

## LEMON AND VODKA MERINGUE CAKE

6 large egg whites
12 oz caster sugar
Custard-6 egg yolks
    4 oz caster sugar
    2 tsp cornflour
    4 fl oz milk
    1 oz butter
juice of 2 - 3 lemons
Vodka cream - 25 fl oz double cream
        3 - 4 tbsp vodka

Whisk together the 6 egg whites and sugar to make the meringue. Use a piping bag and tube to make 20 fingers 2" long and 3 x 5" circles and bake at a low oven temperature for 1 1/2 - 2 hours.

Lemon custard - beat the egg yolks and sugar, fold in 2 tsp cornflour. Heat together the milk and butter until boiling and whisk into the egg mixture. Heat until thickened, stirring occasionally. Add the juice from the lemons.

Vodka cream - whip together the cream and vodka until stiff.

To assemble - alternate layers of meringue circles, custard and cream, and stick the fingers of meringue around the side.

*CHEF'S TIP* - *do not assemble this sweet too soon in advance, as the custard will soften the meringues.*

13

# MENU 7

Smoked Salmon & Cucumber

Veal Swiss

Apple & Hazelnut Meringue

T he starter, slices of smoked salmon with diced cucumber in white wine and cream is served, surprisingly, just warm. The saltiness of the salmon is offset by the sharpness of the white wine and cream sauce.

The main course, which is an escalope of veal pan fried and served with a sauce of Swiss cheee, wine and Kirsch, was inspired by my time in Geneva, when I lingered many a happy evening over a fondue. Partner it with a dry white, such as Frascati.

The dessert, hazelnut, cinnamon and brown sugar meringues, with a layer of lemon-sharpened apple purée, a layer of cream and another of caramelized apples, is a favourite combination of mine, partial as I am to a meringue.

## SMOKED SALMON AND CUCUMBER

8 - 10 oz smoked salmon (thinly sliced)

2 x $1/2$" slices of cucumber (diced)

$1/4$ pt dry white wine

$1/4$ pt cream

$1/4$ pt fish stock

Arrange slices of smoked salmon on your serving plate. Reduce the wine, cream and fish stock in a pan until syrupy. A little cornflour may be needed to adjust consistency at this stage. Add diced cucumber. Warm the smoked salmon briefly in a low oven or under the grill, and pour the sauce on the top. Serve warm.

## VEAL SWISS

**4 veal escalopes, 5 - 6 oz each**
**1/2 pt dry white wine**
**6 oz grated Gruyere cheese**
**6 oz grated Emmenthal or Jarlsberg cheese**
**squeeze of lemon juice**
**2 tbsp Kirsch (or brandy)**
**pepper and nutmeg, to taste**
**2 tsp cornflour**

Sauté the veal very quickly in a little butter and oil - about 2 minutes each side. Set aside and keep warm. Grate the cheeses. Pour the wine into a glass bowl, and add the grated cheese. Microwave, stirring frequently, until the cheese has melted. Mix the cornflour with the Kirsch or brandy, and add to the cheese mixture. Add the squeeze of lemon juice, pepper and nutmeg and heat gently in the microwave until smooth - 2 - 3 minutes, stirring occasionally. The sauce should now be a smooth fondue-consistency. If it is too thick, add a little more wine. To serve, pour the sauce over the escalopes.

*CHEF'S TIP - do not be tempted to substitute the Swiss cheeses with cheddar, as the result will be quite the wrong consistency and flavour.*

## APPLE AND HAZELNUT MERINGUE

**4 oz hazelnuts (roasted and crushed)**
**$^1/_2$ lb soft brown sugar**
**4 egg whites**
**2 tsp ground cinnamon**
**1 $^1/_2$ lb cooking apples (peeled, cored and sliced)**
**1 lemon**
**2 fl oz water**
**3 oz caster sugar**
**1 lb eating apples (peeled and cored)**
**2 oz butter**
**1/2 pt whipped cream (or fromage frais)**

Whisk the egg whites and sugar until stiff, fold in cinnamon. Shape the meringue into 8 ovals, using 2 tablespoons, or a piping bag, onto a baking tray. Sprinkle with the nuts and place in a cool oven 150C/300F/Mark 2 for 1 1/2 - 2 hours. Cook the cooking apples with the rind and juice of the lemon, the water and 1 oz of the caster sugar, until soft. Cut the eating apples into 1/4" thick slices and caramelize in a frying pan with 2 oz caster sugar and the butter.

To assemble:- take 4 serving plates and place 1 meringue on each. Spread a layer of the apple purée, a layer of cream, a layer of caramelized apples, and finish with a meringue on top.

# MENU 8

## Mushrooms & Bacon in Brandy & Cream

## Pork with Gooseberry

## Chocolate Mocha Pot

Mushrooms and Bacon in Brandy and Cream is, as it sounds, a rich and alcoholic starter, served hot and bubbling straight from the grill. A very popular winter starter.

The main course is a pork tenderloin, stuffed with gooseberry and served with a cider sauce. For presentation alone, this dish is excellent, but also the sharpness of the gooseberries is offset very well by the sweetness of the sauce. A New Zealand Sauvignon is the only choice with this dish.

Chocolate Mocha Pot, a rich, dark, chocolate/coffee cream, has to be the Rumbling Tum's most popular sweet. Many times over the years I have tried to remove it from the sweet list, assuming that it had become boring, only to find each time that customer pressure forced its reinstatement.

## MUSHROOMS AND BACON IN BRANDY AND CREAM

1 lb mushrooms (halved)
4 rashers smoked back bacon (roughly diced)
1 clove garlic (finely chopped)
$1/2$ pt cream
2 tbsp brandy
2 oz butter
$1/2$ tsp horseradish
salt and freshly ground pepper
6 oz cheddar cheese (grated)

Lightly sauté the mushrooms in the butter. Remove. Cook the bacon in the same pan. Bring the cream to the boil in a clean pan, and add the garlic. Add the mushrooms and bacon, and reduce. Add the brandy, but do not stir in, and flame with a match if you can, as this will improve the flavour. At this stage you may need to add a little cornflour. Adjust seasoning. Divide the mixture between 4 small oval oven-proof dishes, and sprinkle with cheese. Place under the grill until the cheese is bubbling and golden.

## PORK WITH GOOSEBERRY

2 x 18 oz pork tenderloins
6 oz gooseberries
1 oz sugar
1 oz butter
1 onion (finely chopped)
3 oz wholemeal breadcrumbs
1 tbsp chopped parsley

pinch ground cloves
2 tbsp dry white wine
sauce - $^1/_4$ pt cider
$^1/_4$ pt cream
$^1/_2$ tsp chicken stock
$^1/_4$ pt dry white wine
1 tsp cornflour

Preheat oven to 200C/400F/Gas 6. Top and tail gooseberries. Take 2 oz for garnish and cook with the sugar until tender but not collapsed. Chop the remaining gooseberries. Sauté the onion in the butter over a low heat until transparent, add the gooseberries and cook. Remove from heat and add breadcrumbs, parsley, cloves and wine. Take the tenderloins and cut down each lengthways. Open out flat and flatten with a tenderizer. Spread the stuffing over the meat, roll up and tie in shape with string. Roast in the oven for 45 minutes. Meanwhile, heat the cider, stock and wine together, and add the cream. Reduce. Mix the cornflour with a little water and add to the sauce. Cook for a further 5 minutes.

To serve - cut the tenderloins into 3/4" slices and arrange on top of the sauce on your serving dish. Take the reserved garnish and arrange in the centre of the dish.

## CHOCOLATE MOCHA POT

2 tbsp instant coffee powder or granules
3 oz Bourneville chocolate
$^1/_2$ pt single cream
3 egg yolks
1 $^1/_2$ oz caster sugar

Melt the chocolate with the coffee powder in a glass bowl over a pan of simmering water, stirring occasionally. Bring the cream to the boil and whisk into your chocolate mixture. Whisk together the egg and sugar. Pour the chocolate mixture onto the egg, whisking continuously. Divide between 4 ramekin dishes and stand in a baking tray of hot water in the oven at 120C/ 250F/Gas 2 for 20 - 25 minutes, or until set. Cool, then chill well.

To serve - decorate with cream and chocolate curls.

*CHEF'S TIP - do not allow the chocolate pot to boil in the bain-marie, as this will ruin the texture.*

# MENU 9

**Stuffed Mushrooms**

**Scampi with Ricard**

**Gingered Pears**

Take care in choosing your mushrooms for this starter, they will need to be the larger button-type, not the flat variety, as they are stuffed with Stilton cheese and garlic, and deep-fried in breadcrumbs.

Menu 10's main course is scampi, sauteed with tomato and mushroom, flamed in Ricard and served in a cream and herb sauce - preferably on a bed of rice. An Alsace Riesling would be a good choice of wine with this main course - or even the spicier Gewurztraminer.

Gingered Pears are not as hot as they sound - being pears in an advocaat cream with stem ginger, served chilled. I would suggest serving this sweet with ginger biscuits, or brandy snaps.

## STUFFED MUSHROOMS

**1 lb mushrooms**
**12 - 16 oz stilton**
**breadcrumbs**
**1 clove garlic (finely chopped)**
**3 egg yolks**
**egg wash**

Allow approximately 5 mushrooms per portion. Carefully remove the stalk. Mash the stilton with a fork, incorporate the garlic, and add the egg yolks. Using a small knife, fill the mushroom cavities with the stuffing, and round the top. Dip each mushroom in the egg wash and then the breadcrumbs, to coat evenly. Deep fry in hot oil for about 4 minutes. If the filling starts to splutter before it is cooked, remove and place in a warm oven to finish.

*CHEF'S TIP - ensure that the Stilton mixture is pressed firmly into the mushrooms, or else it will escape during deep-frying.*

## SCAMPI WITH RICARD

**1 lb scampi**
**1 medium-sized tin plum tomatoes**
**3 shallots (chopped finely)**
**6 oz mushrooms (chopped finely)**
**1 oz butter**
**9 oz double cream**
**2 tsp Ricard**
**pinch mixed herbs**

Have all your ingredients ready prepared before you commence cooking, as the scampi takes very little time to cook. Sauté the scampi in the butter with the shallots, herbs, tomatoes, and mushrooms. Pour on the Ricard and flame with a match. Add the double cream and bring to the boil. Remove from heat, season, and serve immediately.

## GINGERED PEARS

**4 ripe William pears**
**$^1/_2$ pt double cream**
**4 fl oz Advocaat**
**2 pieces stem ginger and some syrup**

Peel and dice the pears and divide them between 4 stemmed glasses. Trickle a little ginger syrup over. Whip the cream and Advocaat together until thick and soft. Fold in the chopped stem ginger and spoon over the pears.

*CHEF'S TIP* - *to achieve a spicier result, simply add more of the stem ginger.*

# MENU 10

## Crab Mousse with Smoked Salmon

## Fillet Steak Crownley

## Fruit Basket

T his menu has to be the most sumptuous in this collection, whether you are looking at presentation, flavours or textures.

The starter is a creamy crab mousse, wrapped in smoked salmon, and looks very elegant set on a green leafy garnish - use salad bowl lettuce, endive, green lollo, fennel fronds and a twist of cucumber and lemon.

The Crownley Steak is made up of many different elements - garlic, mushroom, smoked bacon, red wine sauce, and, of course, the steak. The garlic content, 2 cloves in each steak, may seem excessive, but as they are fried, the strength of flavour is arrested somewhat, leaving a smooth creamy taste.

The Fruit Basket is an almond biscuit basket, with a little vanilla ice-cream, and as many different fruits as you are able to find, sliced and displayed on top. The basket is surrounded by a red fruit sauce, and a dusting of icing sugar immediately prior to serving sets off the sweet beautifully.

## CRAB MOUSSE WITH SMOKED SALMON

| | |
|---|---|
| 8 oz crab meat | 1 oz powdered gelatine |
| 2 fl oz double cream | 2 fl oz water |
| 1 tbsp grated Parmesan | a little butter |
| pinch cayenne | 8 oz smoked salmon (thinly |
| 2 tbsp lemon juice | sliced) |
| salt and pepper | 2 egg whites |
| 1 tbsp mayonnaise | |

Add together the crab meat, cheese and cream and blend in a processor until smooth. Add the cayenne, lemon juice and mayonnaise and season. Stir the gelatine into the water and warm gently until dissolved. Set aside to cool. Stir in the crab mixture. Beat the egg whites until frothy and fold into the crab mixture. Take 4 small ramekin dishes, butter them and fill with the crab mixture. Chill until firm.

To serve - turn out onto your garnished serving plates and wrap the slices of smoked salmon around and under each mousse. Serve with a twist of lemon and slices of brown bread and butter.

## FILLET STEAK CROWNLEY

4 x 6 - 8 oz fillet steaks
12 oz mushrooms (finely chopped)
4 oz onion (finely chopped)
2 oz butter
8 rashers smoked back bacon
8 garlic cloves (halved)

Sauce -  1/2 pt red wine
1 beef stock cube
1/2 small onion (chopped)
the juice of 1 segment lemon
1/4 pt cream
2 tsp cornflour

Sweat the onion and mushroom in the butter over a very low heat. Fry the garlic cloves until golden. Take each fillet steak and turn on its side. Make a small incision. Over a high flame quickly colour the steak on all sides to seal. Tuck the garlic cloves into the steak and then stuff with the mushroom duxelle, retaining the shape of the steak. Wrap the rashers of bacon around the steak and secure with cocktail sticks. Cook in a pan or under the grill (on its side) for 8 - 10 minutes, according to taste.

Sauce - combine all the ingredients except the cornflour, and reduce. Thicken with the cornflour and serve.

## FRUIT BASKET

A quantity of Red Fruit Sauce (see Menu 6)
8 tbsp vanilla ice-cream
seasonal fruits as available
icing sugar to dust
baskets - 1 $^1/_2$ egg whites
3 oz icing sugar
2 $^1/_2$ oz unsalted butter
2 $^1/_4$ oz plain flour
few drops almond essence

Preheat oven to 150C/300F/Gas 3. Whisk the egg whites and icing sugar together. Melt the butter. Stir the flour into the egg whites, and fold in the melted butter. Take a non-stick baking tray and spread the mixture into rounds 5" in diameter. Cook until lightly browned. Have 4 upturned glasses or cups standing ready. Using a fish slice, remove the first cooked biscuit and shape very quickly over a cup, to produce an abstract shape. Repeat for all biscuits. Leave to cool. Place in an airtight tin.

To serve - place 2 tbsp of ice-cream in each basket. Slice and arrange fruits decoratively on the top - I would suggest pineapple, grapes, raspberries, peach, strawberries, banana, pear - in fact any fresh fruit available. Pour a little red fruit sauce around each basket. Dust with icing sugar immediately before serving.

*CHEF'S TIP - the biscuit baskets will keep for some time in an airtight tin - but do make sure your container really is airtight, or you will open it to find four very flat almond biscuits!*

# MENU 11

## Lovage & Orange Soup

## Broccoli & Stilton Crumble

## Chocolate Truffle Heart

I make no apology for including lovage here - an ingredient not commonly found. Whilst I appreciate that many readers might not be able to obtain enough of this herb to make the soup - that was just the position I was in a few years ago. But lovage, like many herbs, is very easy to grow, and that is exactly what I did - now it has established quite a large clump, that re-appears every spring. Lovage has such a unique flavour, with a hint of celery. I suggest this soup be served hot, though it would be lovely served chilled on a hot summer's day.

The crumble is an easily prepared vegetarian main course, which can be assembled in advance and reheated.

The sweet is a heart-shaped chocolate truffle, with a secret cherry and Kirsch filling, and surrounded by coffee sauce. If you do not have a heart-shaped mould, any shape with 4 oz capacity will do - though moulds can be obtained from any large kitchen shop.

## LOVAGE AND ORANGE SOUP

**1 doz lovage sprigs**
**1 $^1/_2$ pts chicken stock (or vegetable stock)**
**2 tbsp orange juice**
**1 lemon**
**1 medium onion (chopped)**
**2 tbsp oil**
**pinch nutmeg**
**6 fl oz double cream**

Reserve a few lovage leaves. Sweat the onion in the oil and add the lovage leaves and stalks. Add stock, juice of half the lemon, and orange juice, and blend. Whisk in cream and nutmeg and simmer for 2 minutes. Garnish with slices of lemon and finely chopped lovage.

## BROCCOLI AND STILTON CRUMBLE

2 lb broccoli (fresh or frozen)
sauce -  1 pt milk
         4 tsp cornflour
         4 egg yolks
         8 - 12 oz grated cheddar cheese
topping -   8 oz dried breadcrumbs
         4 oz grated cheddar cheese
         4 oz Stilton cheese

Cook broccoli in a little salted water until tender. Divide between 4 oval-eared heatproof dishes.

Sauce - bring the milk to the boil, add the cornflour and cheese and remove from the heat. Stir in the egg yolks and spread over the broccoli.

Topping - crumble the stilton into the breadcrumbs and cheddar. Mix well and spread over the cheese sauce. Finish under the grill.

## CHOCOLATE TRUFFLE HEARTS

coffee sauce -                 9 oz double cream
   2 egg yolks                 1 tin morello cherry pie filling
   1 oz caster sugar           2 tbsp rum
   1 dstsp powdered coffee     2 tsp Kirsch
   $1/4$ pt milk               3 oz water
9 oz dark chocolate

Sauce - bring the milk to the boil. Whisk egg yolks and sugar and coffee, and add the boiling milk. Cook in the microwave on defrost, stirring occasionally until slightly thickened. Cool and chill.

Mix 2 tbsp of the morello cherries with the Kirsch and set aside to marinade. Melt the chocolate in a glass bowl over a pan of simmering water. Add the water and rum and stir. Remove from heat. Whip the cream until stiff and fold into the warm chocolate. Oil 4 x 4 oz moulds and line with clingfilm. Half-fill each mould with the chocolate mix. Place the marinaded cherries in the centre and cover with the chocolate until the mould is full. Fold the clingfilm over. Chill for 2 hours.

To serve - turn out the chocolate hearts onto your serving plate and remove cling film. Using a knife dipped in hot water, smooth the surface. Pour the coffee sauce around the heart, and dust with cocoa powder. Finally, decorate the corner of each heart with 2 cherries and a chocolate curl.

*CHEF'S TIP - be sure to use a good quality chocolate, such as Bourneville, not cake covering, or else you will not achieve the correct result. If, whilst incorporating the chocolate and cream, the mixture curdles, a short burst in the microwave - 1/2 a minute, will return it to the correct consistency.*

# MENU 12

**Mushrooms Feuilletés**

**Pork with Stilton, Port & Walnuts**

**Gooseberry Trifle**

Mushrooms Feuilletés is a light puff pastry case filled with sliced mushrooms cooked in a white wine and cream sauce. This is a good "standby" dish, as the pastry cases may be prepared in advance and stored, and the filling is very quick to make at the last minute. Double the size of the pastry case to turn this starter into a main course vegetarian dish, and serve with a side salad.

Pork seems to have a natural affinity with Stilton, and in this dish the strength of the cheese and the crunchiness of the walnuts combine with the port to make a very robust sauce.

Whenever trifle is mentioned, do you think of jelly, blancmange, sherry and hundreds and thousands? Banish those thoughts from your mind - this trifle has a base of sponge soaked in Madeira, a layer of gooseberry puree (all pips removed), a layer of rich vanilla custard (made with eggs, not the instant variety) with cream and crushed macaroons on the top.

## MUSHROOMS FEUILLETES

| | |
|---|---|
| 1 lb puff pastry | 3 fl oz white wine |
| 1 lb button mushrooms | 4 fl oz cream |
| 1 oz butter | salt and pepper |
| 1 tsp lemon juice | egg wash |

Preheat oven to 230C/450F/Gas 6. Roll the pastry out into a rectangle 4" x 16", 1/4" thick. Cut into 4 x 4" squares.

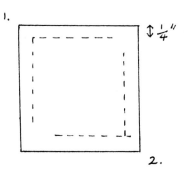

Diagram A                    Diagram B

Cut right through each pastry as per diagram A, along the dotted line. Egg wash the pastry inside the line. Raise points 1. and 2. and cross them over, pressing down firmly onto the egg wash. The result should look like diagram B. Make a diamond pattern on the top and egg wash. Place pastries on a baking tray and cook for 15 - 20 minutes, until golden. Remove from the oven and, using a sharp knife, cut out the centre of each pastry - this will be the lid. Return bases to the oven briefly to dry out.

Sauté the mushrooms in the butter. Add the lemon juice, wine, salt and pepper. Reduce the heat, cover with a lid and cook slowly for 5 minutes. Add the cream and reduce for 10 minutes.

To serve - divide the mushroom mixture between the 4 pastries, filling each one generously. Place the lids on and serve.

## PORK WITH STILTON, PORT AND WALNUTS

2 pork tenderloins, weighing about 2 lb in all
8 fl oz port
2 oz Stilton (crumbled)
2 oz walnuts (chopped)
2 oz onion (finely chopped)
6 fl oz cream
oil and butter to cook

Cut the pork into 8 small steaks and flatten with a tenderizer. Sauté in a frying pan in a little oil and butter for 2 minutes each side. Add the onion and port and reduce. Add the Stilton, cream and walnuts and incorporate well. Serve.

## GOOSEBERRY TRIFLE

1 lb gooseberries
3 oz sugar
8 sponge fingers
6 fl oz cream
2 fl oz Madeira
2 or 3 macaroons

custard - 1 pt milk
3 oz caster sugar
2 tsp vanilla essence
4 egg yolks
1 tsp cornflour

Custard - whisk the egg yolks and sugar in a bowl until almost white, add vanilla essence. Whisk in cornflour. Bring milk to the boil and whisk into the egg yolks, sugar and cornflour and mix well. I would suggest that you use a microwave to bring the custard back to the boil, stirring repeatedly. Set aside to cool.

Cook gooseberries and pass through a sieve. Add the sugar, and cool. Line the base of a glass bowl with the sponge fingers and pour over the Madeira. Pour on the cooled gooseberry purée, followed by the cooled custard. Whip the cream until thick, and spread over the custard. Decorate with the crushed macaroons.

# MENU 13

## Scallops with Strawberries

## Dover Sole Rumbling Tum

## Peaches in Lemon & Brandy

This menu would suit a very special occasion - as the ingredients are on the luxurious side. Care should be taken in assembling the starter - scallops served with mixed salad leaves and a warm strawberry and balsamic vinegar dressing - as it can look either very elegant, or a total mess.

The main course is Dover Sole - the king of salt water fish with all the bones removed - complemented by a prawns and mushroom filling, and a very dramatic presentation. And what else to serve with this but Chablis, lightly chilled.

The peaches are poached in syrup and lemon juice, and marinaded with brandy and I am always disappointed if customers leave the poached lemon slices - they are essential to the full enjoyment of the sweet, and do not taste at all bitter - more akin to the peel in marmalade.

## SCALLOPS WITH STRAWBERRIES

**12 scallops (halved)**
**salad leaves (as many different varieties as you can find)**
**a little lemon juice**
**salt and pepper**
**dressing -**
      **12 oz strawberries**
      **2 tbsp balsamic vinegar**
      **2 fl oz olive oil**

Set aside 4 oz of the smallest of the strawberries, for garnish. Purée the remaining fruit with the vinegar and oil and pass through a sieve. Squeeze a little lemon juice over the scallops, and season lightly. Cook for only 20 - 30 seconds each side. Arrange a small pile of the leaves in the centre of your serving dish. Set the scallops around the edge of the salad, and pour the warmed sauce around.

## DOVER SOLE RUMBLING TUM

4 x 12 - 16 oz Dover Sole (ask your fishmonger to remove the black skin)
8 oz prawns
12 oz mushrooms (sliced)
a little oil and butter
flour to coat
Salt and pepper
dried parsley

Season and flour each fish and brush with a little oil. Place under a hot grill until very lightly coloured. Do not overcook. Sauté the mushrooms in butter and add the prawns, to warm through only at the last minute. Meanwhile, draw a knife down the centre of the cooked fish, then, using a palette knife, ease the top fillets back away from the bone, without breaking and without detaching completely from the fish. Cut through the fish bone just below the head, and again just above the tail, and remove the entire bone, carefully, and reserve. Remove all the small bones along the edge of the fish. Place the mushrooms and prawns along the centre of each fish, and fold the top fillets back, to almost cover the filling. Rinse the bone in water, dip one edge in dried parsley and position, Mohican style, down the length of the fish.

*CHEF'S TIP - if the top fillets do not roll easily back from the bone, or the bone is reluctant to come away from the fish, this will indicate that the fish is not sufficiently cooked - place back under the grill. Have a cup of hot water to hand whilst removing the small bones, to dip your fingers in.*

## PEACHES IN LEMON AND BRANDY

8 large, ripe but firm peaches
2 thinly sliced lemons
8 tsp brandy
1 $^1/_2$ pt water
$^3/_4$ lb sugar

Cook the lemon slices in the water and sugar for about 15 minutes, to make the syrup. Blanch and skin the peaches. Poach the fruit in the syrup until tender. Lift the peaches out, and continue to cook the syrup until it is reduced by half, or until the lemon slices look transparent. Place the peaches in a serving dish. Drizzle a teaspoon of brandy on each peach and pour the reduced syrup over them, including the sliced lemon. Serve chilled.

*CHEF'S TIP - in the unlikely event that you have some peaches and syrup left over, reduce it all in a pan until it becomes the most fruity, alcoholic marmalade I have ever tasted.*

27

# MENU 14

## Brie & Spring Onion Soup

## Venison with Sour Cream & Capers

## Grand Marnier Iced Soufflé

A customer at the Rumbling Tum a short while ago, catching sight of a bowl of Brie and Spring Onion Soup being placed in front of her dinner companion, was heard to say that it was just the delicate pale green colour she was looking for to re-decorate her bedroom! It is a delightful colour, and also a rich flavour, although if you prefer a lighter soup, substitute the cream with milk.

The main course is venison, served with a sour cream and capers sauce. You can, if you prefer buy soured cream to use in this dish, but I prefer to use lemon juice to achieve the same effect with double cream. Menu 1 also features venison, but that is a haunch of venison, and the recipe I give here is for a saddle of venison, which is a superior cut, and should be available if you order it from your butcher. This is not something you are likely to find in your supermarket chill cabinet. The presentation of the saddle is very different - sliced and displayed on top of the sauce. Serve with a glass of Australian Shiraz, or perhaps a Californian Zinfandel.

The dessert is a very light ice-cream soufflé. The cocoa sprinkled on the top gives the effect of a hot dessert, your guests will be surprised to find it is in fact semi-frozen.

## BRIE AND SPRING ONION SOUP

12 oz Brie (chopped coarsely)
1 1/4 pt chicken or vegetable stock
2 oz spring onions (chopped)
4 oz double cream
4 egg yolks
to garnish - 2 oz spring onions

Melt the Brie with the stock in a saucepan over a very low heat. Add the spring onions and cook for 10 minutes until soft. Blend in your liquidizer. Heat the cream almost to boiling point (easiest done in the microwave) and whisk in the egg yolks. Reheat the soup and whisk the cream and egg mixture in, taking care not to boil it. Garnish with finely chopped spring onion.

*CHEF'S TIP - I cannot stress enough that the soup must not be allowed to boil after the addition of the cream and eggs.*

## VENISON WITH SOUR CREAM AND CAPERS

1 $^1/_2$ lb saddle fillet
1 small onion (finely chopped)
$^1/_4$ pt white wine
$^1/_4$ pt beef stock
grated rind and juice of 1 lemon
$^1/_4$ pt cream
small jar capers
salt and pepper

Fry the venison on all sides quickly, for roughly 5 minutes. However, as venison saddles vary so much in thickness, a little more time may be required. Remove meat from the pan and keep warm. In the same pan, add onion, wine and stock and reduce by half. Add lemon juice, cream and capers, and season. Slice the meat into $^1/_4$" slices and arrange on top of the sauce.

*CHEF'S TIP* - *the general rule is to keep the meat rare - medium rare. If it seems to be underdone when sliced, a quick flash under the grill will finish it off. If you prefer your meat well done, this one is not for you.*

## GRAND MARNIER ICED SOUFFLE

4 eggs (separated)
3 oz caster sugar
3 liqueur glasses Grand Marnier
$^1/_2$ pt whipping cream
cocoa to dust

Prepare ramekin dishes by wrapping a 2" greaseproof paper collar around the top of each, and fasten with an elastic band so that the collar stands 1" above the dish. Whisk egg whites with 2 oz of the sugar until stiff but not dry. Whisk egg yolks in a bowl over a pan of hot water with 1 oz sugar until they have doubled in size. Remove from the heat and cool. Whip the cream and fold in the Grand Marnier. Fold the egg yolks into the cream and finally the egg whites. Fill the ramekin dishes to the top of the collar and freeze.

To serve - remove from freezer 10 minutes before serving to soften slightly. Dust with cocoa and remove collar.

# MENU 15

**Kidneys in Red Wine**

**Chicken with Crab & Vermouth**

**Bananas Martinique**

Kidneys, and offal in general, fall into that category of food that you either love or hate - there seems to be no middle ground with them! Reaction of customers to kidneys on the menu at the Rumbling Tum is either one of extreme dislike or rapturous delight. I'm sure our attitude to offal goes back to when we were children - perhaps you can remember being forced to eat liver or kidneys that were terribly overcooked and almost inedible. It is essential not to overcook kidneys, keep them moving round in the pan, over a high heat. Before you include this item on a dinner menu, first check it out with your guests!

Chicken with Crab and Vermouth may seem a strange combination, but it actually works very well together.

What more dramatic way to end a meal than with Bananas Martinique - although you may need to practise your flambé-ing skills before trying it out on your friends.

## KIDNEYS IN RED WINE

1 ¹/₄ lb kidneys
2 shallots (chopped)
¹/₄ pt red wine
¹/₂ beef stock cube
2 oz butter
juice of ¹/₂ lemon
chopped parsley
1 tsp cornflour
a little water

Cut kidneys in half lengthwise, remove gristly parts and slice thinly. Sauté in butter briefly and drain. Keep warm. Add shallots to the pan and cook for a few minutes. Add the wine and beef stock, lemon juice and parsley. Bring to the boil and reduce. Mix the cornflour with a little water and add to the sauce. Cook for a further few minutes.

To serve - divide kidneys between 4 oval-eared dishes and cover with the sauce.

## CHICKEN WITH CRAB AND VERMOUTH

4 chicken breasts (skin, fat and sinew removed)
4 liqueur glasses of vermouth
$^1/_2$ pt cream
4 tbsp crab meat
1 oz butter
2 tsp horseradish
salt and pepper

Cook the chicken gently for 3 - 4 minutes, turn and repeat on the other side without colouring. Add the vermouth to the pan and cook for 3 - 4 minutes with lid on. Season, add the cream and bring to the boil, reducing slightly. Add crab meat and horseradish and heat thoroughly.

To serve - place chicken breasts on serving dish and cover with the sauce.

## BANANAS MARTINIQUE

4 bananas (skinned and split lengthwise)
juice of 1 orange
2 oz butter
3 oz sugar
$^1/_2$ pt apricot jam
2 fl oz rum
flaked, roasted almonds

Caramelize the sugar and butter over a high flame. Add the orange juice and jam and cook for a few seconds. Add the bananas and simmer in the sauce, 3 - 4 minutes. Sprinkle with rum and ignite. As soon as the flame is out, serve the bananas with the sauce on hot plates. Sprinkle with flaked almonds.

# MENU 16

### Deep Fried Camembert

### Salmon with Tomato and Herbs

### Pear, Toffee & Walnut Flan

This starter - camembert breadcrumbed, deep fried, and served with a redcurrant sauce, is a lovely contrast of flavours. Do try and use "lait cru" camembert, to achieve a stronger flavour.

The salmon main course in Menu 2 is sauteed in butter - whereas here we are poaching it in white wine and fish stock - achieving a different texture. The tomato, herb and cream sauce should turn out a light amber colour, speckled with green and red. A crisp Sancerre will prove an admirable partner to this dish.

The dessert is a flan with a biscuit base, a layer of whipped cream, tinned or fresh pears, all covered in a toffee sauce and decorated with walnuts.

## DEEP FRIED CAMEMBERT

**12 - 16 oz camembert (cut into 4 wedges)**
**breadcrumbs**
**egg wash**
**sauce -   1/2 lb redcurrants**
**2 oz caster sugar**
**squeeze lemon juice**
**1 fl oz water**

Sauce - cook, liquidize and sieve the fruit, sugar, lemon juice and water.

Egg and breadcrumb each wedge of camembert twice. Deep fry in hot oil for 3 minutes.

To serve - place one wedge of camembert on each serving plate, and surround with the warmed redcurrant sauce.

## SALMON WITH TOMATO AND HERBS

**4 x 6 oz salmon escalopes**
**$^1/_2$ pt dry white wine**
**4 fl oz water**
**1 tsp fish stock**
**pinch tarragon and parsley**
**4 oz onion (chopped)**
**6 plum tomatoes (seeded and roughly chopped)**
**1 clove garlic (chopped)**
**6 fl oz cream**
**salt and pepper**

Dissolve the fish stock in the wine and water in a deep frying pan with a lid. Add the onion. Place in the salmon and bring to a very slight simmer - the stock should be just trembling. Add the tarragon, parsley, garlic and tomatoes. Place the lid on and poach very lightly for 5 - 8 minutes. Lift the salmon out carefully with a large fish slice on to a warm plate. Add the cream to the poaching liquid and reduce. Adjust seasoning. If the sauce is a little loose, add some cornflour at this stage. Pour the sauce over the salmon and serve.

## PEAR, TOFFEE AND WALNUT FLAN

**12 oz digestive biscuits**
**5 oz butter**
**7 fl oz milk**
**3 oz plain flour**
**12 oz demerara sugar**
**10 oz margarine**
**8 oz walnuts (halved)**
**$^1/_4$ pt whipped cream (unsweetened)**
**4 - 5 pears (halved) - tinned or fresh. If using tinned, drain very well.**

Melt butter, crush biscuits in a liquidizer, mix together, and line the base and sides of a loose-bottomed 10" flan ring.

Toffee - mix flour and milk in a saucepan, add sugar and margarine, and bring slowly to the boil. Set aside to cool.

Line the biscuit base with the whipped cream. Arrange pear halves on top, and spoon the toffee carefully over the top. Chill. Decorate with the halved walnuts.

*CHEF'S TIP - the toffee sauce must be the correct temperature to coat the pears - too warm, and it will run off, too cold and it will be too stiff. Test for consistency by coating one pear only.*

# MENU 17

**Walnut Roulade**

**Mushroom & Leek Feuilletés**

**Edwardian Charlotte**

The walnut roulade is the shape of a swiss roll, but there the similarity ends - the roll of the roulade is crushed walnuts, wrapped around asparagus, quails' eggs and an orange hollandaise sauce. Not one for those counting calories.

The main course is mushrooms and creamed leek in puff pastry, served with a red pepper coulis - a lovely colour and superb fresh taste. Try a rosé wine with this, for a change, perhaps a Cabernet d'Anjou.

Amaretto, the almond-flavoured liqueur, features again in the dessert, teamed with apricots this time, in a light fruity mousse surrounded by boudoir biscuits.

## WALNUT ROULADE

7 oz walnuts
4 eggs
salt and pepper
1 tin asparagus (well drained)
6 quails' eggs (quartered) or 2 hens' eggs
hollandaise sauce -
    zest and juice 1 orange
    3 fl oz white wine vinegar
    6 egg yolks
    6 oz butter
    salt and pepper

Preheat oven to 150C/300F/Gas 3. Process walnuts in a liquidizer until roughly crushed. Whisk eggs and seasoning, and add all but 2 oz of the walnuts. Pour out the mixture on to a non-stick sheet of baking parchment placed on a shallow baking tray 9" x 12". Cook in the oven for 15 minutes until set. Have ready a damp tea towel, and lay a sheet of greaseproof paper on top. Sprinkle the reserved crushed walnuts on to the greaseproof paper and turn out the roulade on top. Press firmly and roll up as a swiss roll, with the greaseproof and tea towel. Leave to cool.

Hollandaise - reduce the orange juice, vinegar and zest in a pan until you are left with only 2 tablespoons. Add this to the egg yolks and whisk in a glass bowl over a pan of hot water. Meanwhile melt the butter in the microwave and whisk in slowly with the eggs until thick. Season and cool.

To assemble - unroll the roulade carefully. Spread the hollandaise in a thick layer over, and evenly distribute the asparagus and eggs. Roll up carefully and chill.

To serve - cut the roulade into 1/2" slices, and allow 2 per portion. Warm slightly in the microwave - it can be served cold, but the flavour and texture improves if slightly warm.

## MUSHROOM AND LEEK FEUILLETS

| | |
|---|---|
| 1 $^1/_2$ lb puff pastry | 8 oz mushrooms (sliced) |
| 1 $^1/_2$ lb leeks | salt and pepper |
| 2 garlic cloves (optional) | 2 red peppers |
| 3 oz butter | 1 tsp sugar |
| $^1/_2$ pt water | cornflour (if required) |
| $^1/_4$ pt cream | |

Prepare 4 puff pastry cases 5" x 5" as shown in menu 13

Sauce - roughly dice the peppers and cook in a little salted water until tender. Add sugar, liquidize and sieve. Thicken with cornflour if required.

Slice leeks, cook with 1oz butter, water and salt, covered, until tender. Add the cream and reduce, adjust seasoning. Cook mushrooms in 2 oz butter and mix into the creamed leek.

To serve - fill the pastry cases with the leek and mushroom mixture, place the pastry top on, and pour the sauce around.

## EDWARDIAN CHARLOTTE

| | |
|---|---|
| 12 oz apricots (stewed or tinned) | 1 tsp vanilla essence |
| $^1/_4$ pt of the juice | 2 tbsp amaretto |
| 1 oz caster sugar | $^1/_2$ pt whipping cream |
| $^1/_2$ oz gelatine | boudoir biscuits |

Cut a circle of greaseproof paper to fit the bottom of a 7" diameter souffle dish (3" in height). Line the mould with the biscuits, flat side inwards. Bring the juice to the boil, dissolve the sugar and gelatine in this. Allow to cool and add the amaretto and essence. Add the apricots and blend as fine as possible. Sieve. Whip the cream and fold into the fruit purée. Pour mixture into the prepared mould and chill. Turn out and serve.

# MENU 18

## Stilton & Apple Strudel

## Sole and Smoked Salmon

## Pink Champagne Sorbet

The starter is a combination of stilton, apple and herbs, wrapped in strudel paste. I learnt the technique for making this paste whilst in Geneva, but it really is not as difficult as it sounds - however you may substitute it with filo pastry, available pre-prepared, if you wish.

Sole and Smoked Salmon is not a cheap dish to prepare although you could use Lemon Sole instead of Dover Sole. The presentation of this main course is quite dramatic, it looks like catherine wheels of pink and white!

And what a luxurious end to a meal - Pink Champagne Sorbet - and what better way to serve it than with thinly sliced fresh peaches.

## APPLE AND STILTON STRUDEL

strudel paste - $^1/_4$ lb flour
$^3/_4$ oz butter or lard
$^1/_2$ a small egg pinch salt
$^1/_8$ - $^1/_4$ pt water as required.
stuffing - 1 lb russet or cox apples
8 oz Stilton cheese
juice 1 lemon
thyme, nutmeg, ground black pepper
4 oz unsalted butter (melted)
4 oz dried breadcrumbs

Strudel paste - beat the egg and about half the water together. Mix with the flour into a soft dough, adding more water if necessary. Work and stretch the mixture until elastic and smooth, gently pulling and coaxing it out until paper thin and almost transparent - use your hands to achieve this result, not a rolling-pin. Brush the pastry with oil, cover and rest for 45 minutes.

Stuffing - chop apples into 1/2" cubes. Place in a bowl and sprinkle with lemon juice. Crumble in Stilton and add thyme and nutmeg. Mix well and season.

Brush strudel paste with butter and sprinkle on a few breadcrumbs. Spread the apple mixture on 2/3 of the pastry leaving a strip uncovered. Roll up. Brush top with remaining butter and sprinkle over breadcrumbs. Bake in preheated oven 200C/400F/Gas 4 for 30 - 35 minutes.

## SOLE AND SMOKED SALMON

3 x 12 oz - 1 lb Dover Sole (filleted - ask your fishmonger to do this for you)
6 slices smoked salmon (cut in half lengthways)
8 fl oz fish stock
8 fl oz dry white wine
8 fl oz double cream
1 tsp cornflour
salt and freshly ground pepper

Flatten the sole fillets lightly on a board. Lay a slice of smoked salmon on top and roll up tightly. Secure with a cocktail stick. Poach the rolls of fish in the stock and wine, cover with a lid, simmering lightly, for about 8 minutes. Lift out the fish and keep warm. Add the cream to the sauce and reduce volume by a third over quite a high heat. Season, thicken with cornflour if necessary.

To serve - divide sauce between 4 serving plates. Remove cocktail sticks from fish rolls and slice each in half, and place on top of the sauce, cut side up, so that the pink of the salmon can be seen.

*CHEF'S TIP* - *keep the addition of salt to the sauce to a minimum, as the salmon will impart a salty flavour of its own.*

## PINK CHAMPAGNE SORBET

9 oz sugar
$1/_2$ pt water
1 tsp ginger syrup (from a jar of stem ginger)
juice 1 orange and 1 lemon
17 fl oz pink champagne
3 egg whites

Bring 5 oz of the sugar, the water, ginger syrup, lemon and orange juices to the boil, cool and mix with champagne. Freeze it - firmer than normal sorbet. Make a meringue of the remaining sugar and the egg whites and fold into the sorbet. Return to freezer. Serve in individual glasses.

# MENU 19

## Crab en Cocotte

## Duck Breast with Chocolate

## Tarte Tatin

This crab starter is particularly useful for the busy hostess, as it can be prepared in advance and frozen. It has a base of sliced mushrooms in port and cream, a layer of crab meat, and a cheesy topping. Serve it hot and bubbling straight from the grill, and add a side salad for a light main course.

The initial reaction of my customers to duck served with chocolate sauce is one of near horror! How ever will these two flavours complement each other? Those brave enough to try it are very pleasantly surprised, as the richness of the duck is offset remarkably well by the bitterness of the chocolate sauce. This is certainly one with which to impress your dinner guests.

Tarte Tatin is the famous upside-down apple tart, named after the proprietors of a French hotel, the Mesdamoiselles Tatin. The story is told of how one of the sisters dropped an apple pie accidentally onto a flagstone floor, scooped it up, upside down, took it back to the kitchen, where it was reheated and served! This recipe does not involve dropping the pie onto the floor. There are many variations on the theme of Tarte Tatin, and I have tried them all. The method I give is the most foolproof I have found.

## CRAB EN COCOTTE

12 oz crab meat
8 oz sliced mushrooms
1 oz butter
2 oz port
2 oz cream
salt, lemon juice
sauce -   1/2 pt milk
          2 tsp cornflour
          2 egg yolks
          4 - 6 oz grated cheddar cheese

Take 4 small cocotte dishes. Soften the sliced mushrooms in butter. Add the port, lemon juice and reduce. Add the cream and boil until thickened. Adjust seasoning. Divide the mixture between the four dishes. Spread the crabmeat on top.

Sauce - bring the milk to the boil, add the cornflour and 2 oz cheese and remove from the heat. Stir in the egg yolks - it should now look like custard - and spread over the crab. Sprinkle on the rest of the grated cheese. Heat for 2 minutes in the microwave, and finish off under the grill.

*CHEF'S TIP - take care to check the white crabmeat for any shell that may be present. If reheating from frozen, heat on low microwave setting to prevent boiling around the edge and spoiling the presentation.*

## DUCK BREAST WITH CHOCOLATE

**4 duck breasts - each 10 - 12 oz**
**cooking oil**
**4 tbsp caster sugar**
**3 fl oz water**
**2 tbsp powdered cocoa (not drinking chocolate)**
**1 tbsp cornflour**
**16 fl oz dry white wine**
**2 tbsp white wine vinegar**
**$^1/_2$ oz butter**
**grated rind of 1 orange**
**to garnish - spiced fruit - peaches or apricots**

Sauce - melt the caster sugar and water in a heavy-bottomed pan. Boil until a light caramel colour. Add 8 fl oz of the wine and all the wine vinegar. Place back on heat and stir until smooth. Stir in the cocoa and cornflour and whisk. Add the butter and the remaining wine, and the orange rind. Reduce the sauce until a medium consistency. This can be made ahead and reheated - if it becomes too thick, add a little more wine.

Take the 4 duck breasts and score the fat with a sharp knife, salt well both sides. Heat the oil in a frying pan and add the duck breasts, keeping over a high heat for 3 minutes, fat side down. Turn over and cook for 2 minutes to seal, and return to the fat side to complete the cooking. This should take another 3 - 4 minutes, according to taste. Remove from pan, leave to rest for a few minutes, and then slice thinly. Arrange the duck in a fan-shape on a serving plate, place the warmed spiced fruit beside it, and pour the reheated sauce in a cordon around the edge.

*CHEF'S TIP - the spiced fruit can be made with either tinned or fresh fruit, soaked in some fruit syrup, to which you have added 1 - 2 cloves, cinnamon and mixed spice.*

*Alternatively, spiced fruit can be purchased from a delicatessen.*

*continued overleaf*

## TARTE TATIN

**6 - 8 dessert apples**
**9 oz puff pastry**
**juice of 1/2 lemon**
**1/2 tsp cinnamon**
**8 oz caster sugar**
**2 oz water**

Put the sugar and water into a heavy-bottomed pan and heat. After 5 minutes approx. you will begin to see colour at the edges. Turn down the heat and swirl the pan around until it develops an amber colour throughout. Leave to cool for 15 minutes. Peel, core and slice the apples. Sprinkle with the lemon juice and cinnamon. Take a round heatproof glass or metal dish 10" in diameter and 2" deep. Spread the cooled caramel over the bottom of the dish, lay the apples on top and cover with the puff pastry. Tuck the pastry in and cook for 20 - 30 minutes on 220C/425F/Mark 8. Turn over carefully when cooked, and all the delicious caramel will be coating the apple, and the pastry will be crisp.

# MENU 20 - Steve Browning's Guest Menu

## Kangaroo Tail Soup

## Stuffed Barramundi

## Pavlova

Steve Browning owned his own restaurant in Australia, and as well as the recipes given here, served crocodile cutlets, balmain bug salad, buffalo casserole, abalone and crow pie (the latter was actually minced beef, herbs and spices, encased in heavy buttered pastry, cooked, apparently, by a "fair dinkum" old crow!) Damper, the original Australian bread, was served with every meal in Steve's restaurant - made by simply mixing plain flour with water to make a dough, to which salt was added. Traditionally, it was shaped into rough rounds, cooked in the hot ashes of a fire, and eaten along with its charred crust.

Kangaroo Tail Soup is perhaps the most famous Australian dish - in the unlikely event that your butcher is unable to supply the main ingredient, you may substitute oxtail.

Australia has a superb variety of fish to choose from - there are over 70 varieties - and the fighting barramundi from North Queensland, cannot be bettered for taste and texture. This fish is available in this country from specialist suppliers - or alternatively you can use cod, hake, bream or haddock.

Controversy continues to rage about the origin of the Australian sweet Pavlova. The most popular and probably true version is that it was invented in Perth by an admiring chef when the Russian dancer Pavlova was touring Western Australia at the turn of the century.

*continued overleaf*

## KANGAROO TAIL SOUP

**2 kangaroo tails**
**a little butter**
**3 carrots**
**sliced 4 onions**
**sliced bunch of herbs**
**l lb gravy beef, sliced**
**salt and pepper**
**5 pts water a little flour, to thicken**

Cut the tails into joints and fry in the butter until they are brown. Add the onions and carrots and fry. Place in a large saucepan with all the other ingredients, bring to the boil and simmer for 4 hours. Remove the tail joints, strain the stock and thicken with flour. Return the joints to the pan and boil for 10 minutes. Serve.

*continued overleaf*

## STUFFED BARRAMUNDI

1 lb barramundi
(ask your fishmonger to remove the head and fins and scale)
juice of 1 lemon
1 green pepper, sliced thinly
2 oz cooked rice
1 stalk celery, finely chopped
1 tsp finely chopped sage leaves
salt and pepper
a little melted butter

Preheat the oven to 180C/350F/Gas 4. Rinse the fish inside and out under cold water, and wipe dry with absorbent paper. Mix together the pepper, rice, celery, onion, sage and lemon juice and season. Stuff the fish with the mixture. Grease a baking dish and place the stuffed fish in it and brush with melted butter. Bake for 35 - 40 minutes, basting occasionally.

## PAVLOVA

4 egg whites
pinch of salt
8 oz caster sugar
1 tsp cornflour
1 tsp vinegar
1 tsp vanilla essence
whipped cream
kiwifruit, passionfruit and strawberries.

Beat the egg whites with the salt until very stiff, gradually blend in the sugar until it is all dissolved. Continue beating and add the cornflour, vinegar and vanilla essence. Pile the mixture thickly on to a 10" tray and bake near the bottom of the oven at 140C/275F/Gas 2 for about 1 1/2 hours or until quite firm to the touch. Turn the heat off and leave the pavlova in the oven until cool. Fill with whipped cream and garnish with the fruit.

# ACKNOWLEDGEMENTS

Steve Browning, for his encouragement and for believing in the cuisine that I serve.

Frances, for compiling the menus — for several hours spent patiently (?!) following me round the kitchen trying to extract exact quantities of ingredients, etc., and several more sat at the typewriter.

Adrian, for his humorous cartoon drawings, and Chris, for his meticulous proof-reading.

Christine Branson, for the loan of her wordprocessor